Yaprendí

A Guided Journal for Spanish Language Learners

PART 1

CHRISTINA GOLSON

FAIR USE DISCLAIMER
For any copyrighted visuals seen throughout this work:

Copyright Disclaimer under section 107 of the Copyright Act of 1976, allowance is made for "fair use" for purposes such as criticism, comment, news reporting, teaching, scholarship, education and research.

Fair use is a use permitted by copyright statute that might otherwise be infringing.

YAPRENDÍ SOCIETY LLC

BEHIND THE NAME
YAPRENDÍ

Yaprendí, was derived from the Spanish phrase
"Ya aprendí", which roughly translates to "Now I've learned!"

"Ya" means "now" or "already".
"Aprendí" comes from the verb "aprender", which means "to learn".
"Prendí" comes from the verb "prender"
- roughly meaning "to ignite".
With this in mind, Yaprendí can also be interpreted as "Now I'm ignited!"
Or, "I've turned (something) on!"— in this case, new language skills!

The inspiration behind the name for Yaprendí Society is the following life lesson:
When you let life's diversity spark your curiosity to learn more, you never stop growing.

YAPRENDÍ MISSION

Yaprendí seeks to empower Spanish language learners of all ages and from all cultural backgrounds to develop language skills that will increase their confidence in communication and promote a deeper curiosity in linguistic differences. We seek to expand our cultural awareness in a way that will enable us to make meaningful connections and become better global citizens. We are a society of life-long learners who genuinely value and respect each other's diverse differences and understand that we each have a uniqueness that contributes to the beauty of our world.
This perspective fosters a growth mindset,
and progressive thinking to help advance ourselves as individuals-
thereby advancing our society as a whole.

Introduction

¡HOLA YAPRENDIZ! THANK YOU FOR INVESTING IN THIS JOURNAL AND INVESTING IN YOURSELF BY WORKING TO IMPROVE YOUR SPANISH SKILLS. YOU ARE ON YOUR WAY TO ACHIEVING YOUR SPANISH FLUENCY GOALS!
¡UN APLAUSO!

LEARNING A NEW LANGUAGE IS A LIFE-LONG PROCESS. AS A PERSON WHO HAS STARTED FROM ZERO AND ACHIEVED NEAR-NATIVE FLUENCY IN SPANISH OVER THE COURSE OF 20 YEARS, I WANTED TO CREATE A TOOL THAT COULD HELP OTHERS ALONG THEIR JOURNEY TO ACHIEVE SIMILAR LIFE-ENHANCING RESULTS. I DESIGNED THIS JOURNAL TO BE BENEFICIAL AT ANY STAGE OF LANGUAGE LEARNING- WITH THE UNDERSTANDING IN MIND THAT THERE IS ALWAYS MORE TO LEARN. FOR THAT REASON, WHETHER YOU ARE A BEGINNER, INTERMEDIATE OR ADVANCED LEARNER, YOU CAN EQUALLY BENEFIT FROM USING THIS JOURNAL!

ONE OF THE THINGS THAT HELPED ME ALONG MY LANGUAGE LEARNING JOURNEY WAS WRITING DAILY JOURNAL ENTRIES IN SPANISH. NO MATTER HOW POOR I PERCEIVED MY LANGUAGE SKILLS TO BE, I WOULD ALWAYS PUSH MYSELF TO EXPRESS MY THOUGHTS THE BEST I COULD, ONLY IN SPANISH.

DUE TO THIS LEVEL OF UNWAVERING DEDICATION, I HAVE HAD THE PRIVILEGE OF BEING ABLE TO EXPERIENCE LIFE MORE ABUNDANTLY THROUGH MAKING MEANINGFUL CONNECTIONS WITH PEOPLE ALL OVER THE WORLD IN THE SPANISH LANGUAGE.

STEPPING OUT OF MY COMFORT ZONE TO MAKE THIS HAPPEN HAS MADE MY LIFE SO MUCH MORE FULFILLING THAN IT WOULD HAVE BEEN OTHERWISE- AND I WANT TO SHARE THAT EXPERIENCE WITH YOU! THE KEY IS TO NEVER GIVE UP AND NEVER STOP LEARNING. IGNITE YOUR PASSION AND CURIOSITY AND GET COMFORTABLE WITH BEING UNCOMFORTABLE.

THIS JOURNAL IS PART 1 OF A SERIES OF 4 GUIDED JOURNALS THAT ARE DESIGNED TO BE COMPLETED OVER THE COURSE OF A YEAR. EACH PART OF THE SERIES CONTAINS A TOTAL OF 13 PROMPTS. FEEL FREE TO BEGIN AT ANY POINT IN THE YEAR.

WHILE EACH PROMPT REQUIRES A WRITTEN RESPONSE, EACH WEEK YOU WILL PLACE INCREASED EMPHASIS ON ONE OF THE FOUR LANGUAGE LEARNING MODALITIES IN THE FOLLOWING SEQUENTIAL CYCLE:
WRITING, READING, LISTENING AND SPEAKING.

THE IDEA IS TO COMPLETE A DIFFERENT PROMPT EACH WEEK. EVERY SPANISH SPEAKING COUNTRY IS REPRESENTED AT LEAST ONCE THROUGHOUT THE ENTIRE SERIES OF GUIDED JOURNALS AS A CULTURAL THEME FOR CORRESPONDING PROMPTS. YOU MAY CHOOSE TO SELECT A CULTURAL FOCUS ACCORDING TO YOUR PERSONAL INTERESTS FOR ANY WEEKS THAT DO NOT SPECIFY A COUNTRY.

YOU CAN COMPLETE THE PROMPTS AT ANY PACE THAT YOU PREFER. MAKE THIS JOURNAL YOUR OWN AND DO WHAT FEELS RIGHT FOR YOU!

TREAT THIS BOOK LIKE YOUR LANGUAGE-LEARNING DIARY. REFLECT ON YOUR PROGRESS AND KEEP PUSHING YOURSELF TO ALWAYS ACHIEVE BETTER, BECAUSE YOU REALLY CAN!

FEEL FREE TO ALTER THE PROMPTS TO YOUR LIKING.
MY ONLY ASK IS THAT YOU COMMIT TO DEVELOPING YOUR SKILLS AND DOCUMENTING YOUR JOURNEY ALONG THE WAY IN THIS JOURNAL. I PROMISE YOU WILL BE SO PROUD OF HOW FAR YOU'LL HAVE COME!

THANK YOU FOR JOINING THE YAPRENDÍ SOCIETY!

YOU ARE ENCOURAGED TO USE SUGGESTED ONLINE RESOURCES AND TEXTS TO DOCUMENT THE MOST ESSENTIAL INFORMATION YOU WILL NEED BASED ON YOUR LEARNING LEVEL.

THIS METHOD WILL BETTER ASSIST YOU IN RETAINING THE NEW INFORMATION YOU ARE LEARNING. BEFORE YOU BEGIN, DOWNLOAD THE FOLLOWING APPS ON YOUR PHONE AND/OR BOOKMARK THE WEBSITES ON YOUR DEFAULT WEB BROWSER.

Week 1: ¿Quién Eres?

THIS WEEK IS ALL ABOUT DESCRIBING YOURSELF IN SPANISH. CHALLENGE YOURSELF TO WRITE AT LEAST 5-10 SENTENCES OR MORE FOR EACH ENTRY, ACCORDING TO YOUR LEARNING LEVEL. USE SUGGESTED APPS/ ONLINE RESOURCES TO LOOK UP UNFAMILIAR WORDS.

Complete these activities according to your learning level. The more advanced your learning level, the more detailed your responses should be.

1. ¿Quién eres y cómo es tu personalidad?

2. ¿A qué te dedicas diariamente? ¿Trabajas? ¿Eres estudiante? ¿Ambos? Explica.

3. Describe el día perfecto para ti. ¿Dónde estarías? ¿Qué cosas harías? ¿Con quiénes estarías?

 4. Describe tu comida preferida.

5. Describe tu ciudad natal con mucho detalle.

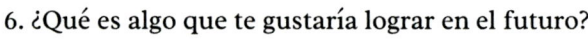 6. ¿Qué es algo que te gustaría lograr en el futuro?

 7. Nombra un país hispanohablante que te gustaría visitar. ¿Por qué? ¿Qué actividades te gustaría hacer allí?

*JOURNAL ENTRY PAGES BEGIN AFTER HELPFUL RESOURCES AND NOTE-TAKING PAGES LABELED "APUNTES"

HELPFUL SENTENCE STARTERS:

YO SOY…	I AM… (PROFESSION/ PERSONALITY)
MI NOMBRE ES…	MY NAME IS
SOY DE…	I AM FROM…
ME GUSTA…	I LIKE …
MI PLATO PREFERIDO ES…	MY FAVORITE DISH IS…
MI DÍA PERFECTO SERÍA…	MY PERFECT DAY WOULD BE…
ME GUSTARÍA LOGRAR… EN EL FUTURO	I WOULD LIKE TO ACHIEVE…. IN THE FUTURE…
UN PAÍS QUE ME GUSTARÍA VISITAR ES… PORQUE…	A COUNTRY I WOULD LIKE TO VISIT IS… BECAUSE…
MI CIUDAD NATAL ES…	MY BIRTH CITY/ HOMETOWN IS…

HELPFUL SENTENCE STARTERS:

ME LLEVO BIEN CON...	I GET ALONG WELL WITH...
ALGO MUY IMPORTANTE PARA MÍ ES...	SOMETHING VERY IMPORTANT TO ME IS...
CREO QUE ...	I BELIEVE THAT...
YO SÉ (VERB IN SPANISH).....	I KNOW (HOW TO) (VERB IN SPANISH)...
MIS PASATIEMPOS FAVORITOS SON...	MY FAVORITE PASTIMES ARE...
ME DA ENERGÍA (VERB IN SPANISH)...	IT ENERGIZES ME TO (VERB IN SPANISH)...
ES DIFÍCIL (VERB IN SPANISH)	IT'S DIFFICULT TO (VERB IN SPANISH)
ES FÁCIL (VERB IN SPANISH)...	IT'S EASY TO (VERB IN SPANISH)...
LAS ACTIVIDADES QUE MÁS ME GUSTAN SON...	THE ACTIVITIES I LIKE THE MOST ARE...

USEFUL PREPOSITIONS & ADVERBS:

A	AT / TO
ANTES (DE)	BEFORE
A TRAVÉS DE	THROUGH
ARRIBA (DE)	ABOVE
BAJO (DE)	UNDER
CON	WITH
CONTRA	AGAINST
DE	OF / FROM
DEBAJO DE	UNDERNEATH
DETRÁS DE	BEHIND
DESDE	FROM / SINCE
DESPUÉS (DE)	AFTER
DENTRO DE	INSIDE / WITHIN
DURANTE	DURING

USEFUL PREPOSITIONS & ADVERBS:

EN	IN
ENCIMA DE	ON TOP OF
ENTRE	AMONG/ BETWEEN
HACIA	TOWARDS
HASTA	UNTIL
JUNTO A	NEXT TO
PARA	FOR/ IN ORDER TO
POR	FOR/ BY/ BY WAY OF
SIN	WITHOUT
SEGÚN	ACCORDING TO
SOBRE	ON (TOP OF)

SOBRE ALSO MEANS ENVELOPE, JUST DEPENDS ON CONTEXT

Common Adjectives and Verbs

Adjectives: divertida(o) [fun], interesante [interesting], reservada(o) [shy/reserved], deportista [athletic], estudioso(a) [studious], inteligente [intelligent], trabajador(a) [hard-working], sociable [social], aventurero(a)/atrevida(o) [adventurous/daring], tranquila(o) [calm/peaceful], alto(a) [tall], baja(o) [short], artística(o) [artistic], alegre [happy/joyful], realista [realistic], práctico(a) [practical], aburrida(o) [boring], curioso(a) [curious], feo(a) [ugly], linda(o) [pretty], simpático(a) [nice/kind], antipático(a) [mean/unpleasant]

NOTE: GENERALLY SPEAKING, **ADJECTIVES** ENDING IN -O REFER TO A MASCULINE SUBJECT- WHILE THOSE ENDING IN -A REFER TO A FEMININE ONE. IT IS IMPORTANT TO NOTE THAT THERE ARE SOME EXCLUSIONS TO THIS RULE THAT YOU WILL LEARN THROUGHOUT YOUR SPANISH LEARNING JOURNEY. ALSO, THESE DAYS, IT IS COMMON TO REPLACE EITHER -A OR -O WITH AN -E WHEN REFERING TO A GENDER -NEUTRAL OR NON-BINARY INDIVIDUAL.

Cocinar — to cook

Bailar — to dance

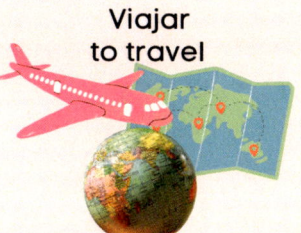
Viajar — to travel

Escuchar música — to listen to music

Pintar — to paint

Ver películas / Ir al cine — to watch movies / to go to the movies

Dibujar — to sketch

Jugar deportes — to play sports

Salir con amigos — to go out with friends

Hacerse maquillaje — to do makeup

Ir de compras — to go shopping

Common Professions in Spanish

Doctor / Médico(a)
Doctor

Cocinero (a)
cook

Bailarín(a)
dancer

Profesor(a) / Maestro (a)
Teacher

Consultor (a)
Consultant

Obrero (a) (de construcción)
Construction worker

Agente de Viajes
Travel agent

Banquero (a)
Banker

Director(a) de Programas
Director of programs

Gerente / Jefe (a)
Manager / Boss

Reportero (a) / Corresponsal
News Reporter

Abogado(a)
lawyer

Artista
artist

Cajera(o)
cashier

deportista
athlete

PRO TIP:
Take note of the 2 most helpful verb conjugation endings and a few Spanish words you may need to refer back to as you complete this week's prompt

VERB TENSE:		
PRONOUNS:	AR VERBS	ER/IR VERBS
YO:		
TÚ		
ÉL, ELLA, USTED		
NOSOTROS (AS)		
VOSOTROS(AS) SPAIN ONLY		
USTEDES, ELLOS, ELLAS		

VERB TENSE:		
PRONOUNS:	AR VERBS	ER/IR VERBS
YO:		
TÚ		
ÉL, ELLA, USTED		
NOSOTROS (AS)		
VOSOTROS(AS) SPAIN ONLY		
USTEDES, ELLOS, ELLAS		

PARTS OF SPEECH:
N = NOUN
V = VERB
ADV = ADJVERB
ADJ = ADJECTIVE
PREP = PREPOSITION

JAN	FEB	MAR	APR	MAY	JUN	JUL	AUG	SEP	OCT	NOV	DEC

1 2 3 4 5 6 7 8 9 10 11 12 13 14 15 16 17 18 19 20 21 22 23 24 25 26 27 28 29 30 31

| JAN | FEB | MAR | APR | MAY | JUN | JUL | AUG | SEP | OCT | NOV | DEC |

1 2 3 4 5 6 7 8 9 10 11 12 13 14 15 16 17 18 19 20 21 22 23 24 25 26 27 28 29 30 31

| JAN | FEB | MAR | APR | MAY | JUN | JUL | AUG | SEP | OCT | NOV | DEC |

1 2 3 4 5 6 7 8 9 10 11 12 13 14 15 16 17 18 19 20 21 22 23 24 25 26 27 28 29 30 31

| JAN | FEB | MAR | APR | MAY | JUN | JUL | AUG | SEP | OCT | NOV | DEC |

1 2 3 4 5 6 7 8 9 10 11 12 13 14 15 16 17 18 19 20 21 22 23 24 25 26 27 28 29 30 31

| JAN | FEB | MAR | APR | MAY | JUN | JUL | AUG | SEP | OCT | NOV | DEC |

1 2 3 4 5 6 7 8 9 10 11 12 13 14 15 16 17 18 19 20 21 22 23 24 25 26 27 28 29 30 31

| JAN | FEB | MAR | APR | MAY | JUN | JUL | AUG | SEP | OCT | NOV | DEC |

1 2 3 4 5 6 7 8 9 10 11 12 13 14 15 16 17 18 19 20 21 22 23 24 25 26 27 28 29 30 31

JAN	FEB	MAR	APR	MAY	JUN	JUL	AUG	SEP	OCT	NOV	DEC

1 2 3 4 5 6 7 8 9 10 11 12 13 14 15 16 17 18 19 20 21 22 23 24 25 26 27 28 29 30 31

WEEKLY CHECK IN

DATE: _____

3 NEW VERBS I LEARNED THIS WEEK:
- _____
- _____
- _____

A LANGUAGE LEARNING CHALLENGE I HAD THIS WEEK:

OVERALL, MY SPANISH FELT LIKE:

NEXT WEEK I WANT TO IMPROVE
_____
_____
_____
_____

THINGS I ACCOMPLISHED THIS WEEK

MY FAVORITE THING I LEARNED THIS WEEK

MY SPANISH WRITING THIS WEEK
☆ ☆ ☆ ☆ ☆

🇪🇸 Week 2: Lectura sobre España

THIS WEEK, READ AND LEARN SOMETHING NEW ABOUT SPAIN.
CHOOSE ONE OF THE FOLLOWING ONLINE RESOURCES TO FIND A SPANISH READING ACCORDING TO YOUR CURRENT LEVEL.

WRITE AT LEAST 4 JOURNAL ENTRIES SUMMARIZING NEW HISTORICAL OR CULTURAL FACTS YOU LEARN IN 5-10 SENTENCES OR MORE IN SPANISH.

Beginner (A1-A2):   (ENGLISH) BRITANNICA.COM/PLACE/SPAIN

- **LINGUA.COM** (GO TO "ESPAÑOL" AND SCROLL TO NIVEL A1. SELECT A TEXT)
- **SPANISH.KWIZIQ.COM** (ADD ON /LEARN/READING/GIJON FOR SUGGESTED READING)
- **LEARNPRACTICALSPANISHONLINE.COM** (CLICK BEGINNER ON THE LEFT, THEN BEGINNER PRACTICE READINGS. SELECT A READING)

Intermediate (B1-B2)

- **LINGUA.COM** (GO TO "ESPAÑOL" AND SCROLL TO NIVEL B1. SELECT A TEXT)
- **INMSOL.COM** (GO TO SPANISH EXERCISES- READING COMPREHENSION)
- **DELEAHORA.COM** (SCROLL TO ACTIVIDADES Y RECURSOS- COMPRENSIÓN DE LECTURA)

Advanced (C1-C2)

- **LAMONCLOA.GOB.ES**
- **CERVANTES.ES**
- **ELPAÍS.ES**

HELPFUL SENTENCE STARTERS:

HOY LEÍ SOBRE...	TODAY I READ ABOUT...
LA LECTURA SE TITULA...	THE READING IS TITLED...
LA LECTURA SE TRATA DE...	THE READING IS ABOUT...
ALGO INTERESANTE QUE APRENDÍ FUE QUE...	SOMETHING INTERESTING THAT I LEARNED WAS...
ME CUESTA ENTENDER QUE...	IT'S CHALLENGING FOR ME TO UNDERSTAND THAT...
LA CULTURA ESPAÑOLA ME PARECE...	TO ME, SPANISH CULTURE SEEMS...
LA PARTE MÁS INTERESANTE FUE...	THE MOST INTERESTING PART WAS...
ME GUSTA LA IDEA DE QUE...	I LIKE THE IDEA THAT...
NO ME GUSTA EL HECHO DE QUE...	I DON'T LIKE THE FACT THAT...

PRO TIP:
USE THE FOLLOWING STRATEGIES WHEN READING IN SPANISH:

1. CONTEXTO: INFER MEANING OF UNFAMILIAR WORDS FROM THE CONTEXT THAT YOU ARE ABLE TO COMPREHEND.

2. COGNADO: IDENTIFY COGNATES OR WORDS THAT LOOK FAMILIAR TO YOU FOR THEIR SIMILARITY IN SOUND OR SPELLING IN BOTH ENGLISH AND SPANISH. (FOR EXAMPLE, IMPORTANT AND IMPORTANTE ARE COGNATES)

3. FAMILIA DE PALABRAS: IDENTIFY WORD FAMILIES OR WORDS THAT LOOK SIMILAR TO WORDS YOU ALREADY KNOW. FOR EXAMPLE:
CALOR, CALENTAR, CALIENTE ALL HAVE TO DO WITH HEAT AND THEY BELONG TO THE SAME WORD FAMILY WITH THEIR PREFIX -CAL

JAN	FEB	MAR	APR	MAY	JUN	JUL	AUG	SEP	OCT	NOV	DEC

1 2 3 4 5 6 7 8 9 10 11 12 13 14 15 16 17 18 19 20 21 22 23 24 25 26 27 28 29 30 31

JAN	FEB	MAR	APR	MAY	JUN	JUL	AUG	SEP	OCT	NOV	DEC

1 2 3 4 5 6 7 8 9 10 11 12 13 14 15 16 17 18 19 20 21 22 23 24 25 26 27 28 29 30 31

| JAN | FEB | MAR | APR | MAY | JUN | JUL | AUG | SEP | OCT | NOV | DEC |

1 2 3 4 5 6 7 8 9 10 11 12 13 14 15 16 17 18 19 20 21 22 23 24 25 26 27 28 29 30 31

| JAN | FEB | MAR | APR | MAY | JUN | JUL | AUG | SEP | OCT | NOV | DEC |

1 2 3 4 5 6 7 8 9 10 11 12 13 14 15 16 17 18 19 20 21 22 23 24 25 26 27 28 29 30 31

| JAN | FEB | MAR | APR | MAY | JUN | JUL | AUG | SEP | OCT | NOV | DEC |

1 2 3 4 5 6 7 8 9 10 11 12 13 14 15 16 17 18 19 20 21 22 23 24 25 26 27 28 29 30 31

| JAN | FEB | MAR | APR | MAY | JUN | JUL | AUG | SEP | OCT | NOV | DEC |

1 2 3 4 5 6 7 8 9 10 11 12 13 14 15 16 17 18 19 20 21 22 23 24 25 26 27 28 29 30 31

WEEKLY CHECK IN

DATE: _____

3 NEW WORDS I LEARNED THIS WEEK:
- _____
- _____
- _____

A LANGUAGE LEARNING CHALLENGE I HAD THIS WEEK:

OVERALL, MY SPANISH FELT LIKE:

NEXT WEEK I WANT TO IMPROVE
_____
_____
_____
_____

THINGS I ACCOMPLISHED THIS WEEK

MY FAVORITE THING I LEARNED THIS WEEK

MY SPANISH READING THIS WEEK
★ ★ ★ ★ ★

Week 3: Podcast en Español

Choose one of the following podcasts to listen to every day this week. Summarize something new you learned from your selected podcast in Spanish for each journal entry.

Search for topics related to Spain as your cultural focus.

To make your learning more intensive, make this a part of your daily routine throughout the year. You can find these podcasts on Spotify or Apple Podcasts.

- **Spanish from Zero**
- **Duolingo Spanish Podcast**
- **Latin ELE Speaking Spanish for Beginners**

- **News in Slow Spanish**
- **Chill Spanish Listening Practice**
- **Learn Spanish with Stories**

- **Nómadas**
- **CNN 5 Cosas**
- **Noticias ONU**
- **Noticias Telemundo en la Noche**

Apuntes

PRO TIP:

LISTENING STRATEGIES THAT WILL HELP YOU ALONG YOUR JOURNEY:

1. LISTEN CLOSELY AND REPEAT WHAT YOU HEAR TO YOURSELF OFTEN
2. REPLAY THE AUDIO WHEN YOU DON'T UNDERSTAND- DON'T BE ASHAMED OF HOW LONG IT MAY TAKE, REPETITION IS INTERNALIZATION
3. TAKE NOTES TO GO BACK TO NEW INFORMATION

| JAN | FEB | MAR | APR | MAY | JUN | JUL | AUG | SEP | OCT | NOV | DEC |

1 2 3 4 5 6 7 8 9 10 11 12 13 14 15 16 17 18 19 20 21 22 23 24 25 26 27 28 29 30 31

| JAN | FEB | MAR | APR | MAY | JUN | JUL | AUG | SEP | OCT | NOV | DEC |

1 2 3 4 5 6 7 8 9 10 11 12 13 14 15 16 17 18 19 20 21 22 23 24 25 26 27 28 29 30 31

| JAN | FEB | MAR | APR | MAY | JUN | JUL | AUG | SEP | OCT | NOV | DEC |

1 2 3 4 5 6 7 8 9 10 11 12 13 14 15 16 17 18 19 20 21 22 23 24 25 26 27 28 29 30 31

| JAN | FEB | MAR | APR | MAY | JUN | JUL | AUG | SEP | OCT | NOV | DEC |

1 2 3 4 5 6 7 8 9 10 11 12 13 14 15 16 17 18 19 20 21 22 23 24 25 26 27 28 29 30 31

JAN	FEB	MAR	APR	MAY	JUN	JUL	AUG	SEP	OCT	NOV	DEC

1 2 3 4 5 6 7 8 9 10 11 12 13 14 15 16 17 18 19 20 21 22 23 24 25 26 27 28 29 30 31

| JAN | FEB | MAR | APR | MAY | JUN | JUL | AUG | SEP | OCT | NOV | DEC |

1 2 3 4 5 6 7 8 9 10 11 12 13 14 15 16 17 18 19 20 21 22 23 24 25 26 27 28 29 30 31

WEEKLY CHECK IN

DATE: _____

3 NEW WORDS I LEARNED THIS WEEK:

- _____
- _____
- _____

A LANGUAGE LEARNING CHALLENGE I HAD THIS WEEK:

OVERALL, MY SPANISH FELT LIKE:

NEXT WEEK I WANT TO IMPROVE

_____
_____
_____
_____

THINGS I ACCOMPLISHED THIS WEEK

MY FAVORITE THING I LEARNED THIS WEEK

MY SPANISH LISTENING THIS WEEK

★ ★ ★ ★ ★

Week 4: Pedir Comida

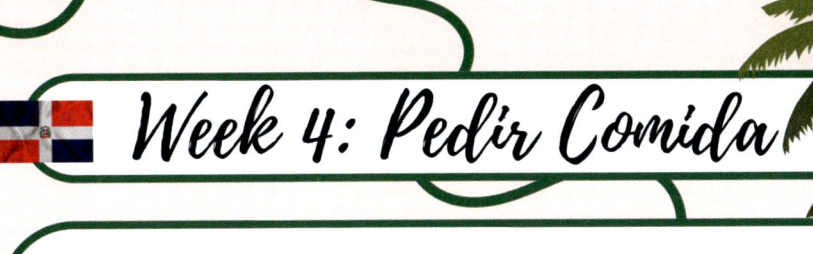

THE CULTURAL FOCUS THIS WEEK IS THE BEAUTIFUL DOMINICAN REPUBLIC!

¡TIENES QUE PEDIR COMIDA EN ESPAÑOL!
THIS WEEK IS ALL ABOUT GETTING SOME SPEAKING PRACTICE WHILE USING THE CONTEXT OF ORDERING FOOD!

YOUR TASK IS TO DO A GOOGLE SEARCH OR USE A RESOURCE BELOW TO LOOK UP A NEW RECIPE IN DOMINICAN CUISINE.

IN YOUR JOURNAL ENTRIES, TALK ABOUT DIFFERENT DISHES IN SPANISH. BE SURE TO ALSO INCLUDE HOW YOU WOULD ORDER THESE MEALS IN SPANISH AND PRACTICE SAYING IT OUT LOUD!

ON THE LAST DAY OF THE WEEK, FIND A DOMINICAN RESTAURANT WHERE YOU CAN ACTUALLY ORDER A DISH THAT APPEALS TO YOU IN SPANISH. IF THIS IS NOT AN OPTION FOR YOU, PRACTICE WITH A FRIEND INSTEAD- CREATE THE SCENARIO AND HAVE FUN WITH IT!

DOCUMENT YOUR PROGRESS ALONG THE WAY AND REMEMBER NOT TO TAKE YOURSELF TOO SERIOUSLY!

SUGGESTED RESOURCES

NOMADPARADISE.COM/DOMINICAN-FOOD/

COCINADOMINICANA.COM/

GODOMINICANREPUBLIC.COM/ES/SOBRE-RD/GASTRONOMIA/

| JAN | FEB | MAR | APR | MAY | JUN | JUL | AUG | SEP | OCT | NOV | DEC |

1 2 3 4 5 6 7 8 9 10 11 12 13 14 15 16 17 18 19 20 21 22 23 24 25 26 27 28 29 30 31

| JAN | FEB | MAR | APR | MAY | JUN | JUL | AUG | SEP | OCT | NOV | DEC |

1 2 3 4 5 6 7 8 9 10 11 12 13 14 15 16 17 18 19 20 21 22 23 24 25 26 27 28 29 30 31

JAN	FEB	MAR	APR	MAY	JUN	JUL	AUG	SEP	OCT	NOV	DEC

1 2 3 4 5 6 7 8 9 10 11 12 13 14 15 16 17 18 19 20 21 22 23 24 25 26 27 28 29 30 31

| JAN | FEB | MAR | APR | MAY | JUN | JUL | AUG | SEP | OCT | NOV | DEC |

1 2 3 4 5 6 7 8 9 10 11 12 13 14 15 16 17 18 19 20 21 22 23 24 25 26 27 28 29 30 31

| JAN | FEB | MAR | APR | MAY | JUN | JUL | AUG | SEP | OCT | NOV | DEC |

1 2 3 4 5 6 7 8 9 10 11 12 13 14 15 16 17 18 19 20 21 22 23 24 25 26 27 28 29 30 31

| JAN | FEB | MAR | APR | MAY | JUN | JUL | AUG | SEP | OCT | NOV | DEC |

1 2 3 4 5 6 7 8 9 10 11 12 13 14 15 16 17 18 19 20 21 22 23 24 25 26 27 28 29 30 31

| JAN | FEB | MAR | APR | MAY | JUN | JUL | AUG | SEP | OCT | NOV | DEC |

1 2 3 4 5 6 7 8 9 10 11 12 13 14 15 16 17 18 19 20 21 22 23 24 25 26 27 28 29 30 31

WEEKLY CHECK IN

DATE: _____

3 NEW WORDS I LEARNED THIS WEEK:
- _____
- _____
- _____

A LANGUAGE LEARNING CHALLENGE I HAD THIS WEEK:

OVERALL, MY SPANISH FELT LIKE:

NEXT WEEK I WANT TO IMPROVE
_____
_____
_____
_____

THINGS I ACCOMPLISHED THIS WEEK

MY FAVORITE THING I LEARNED THIS WEEK

MY SPANISH SPEAKING THIS WEEK
★ ★ ★ ★ ★

Week 5: La Gramática

LET'S POLISH UP ON OUR SPANISH GRAMMAR THIS WEEK!

WHILE HAVING PERFECT GRAMMAR IS NOT ESSENTIAL TO COMMUNICATION IN LANGUAGE LEARNING, IT DEFINITELY HELPS TO KNOW THE LANGUAGE RULES TO ENHANCE YOUR KNOWLEDGE AND UNDERSTANDING OF THE LANGUAGE.

THIS WEEK, FOCUS ON ONE PARTICULAR GRAMMAR TOPIC THAT YOU KNOW YOU COULD IMPROVE UPON. USE WORDREFERENCE, SPANISHDICT AND/OR OTHER ONLINE RESOURCES TO TAKE NOTES ON GRAMMAR RULES. IN YOUR JOURNAL ENTRIES, DOCUMENT YOUR THOUGHTS ABOUT YOUR CURRENT GRAMMAR FOCUS WITH EXAMPLES OF HOW TO USE THE RULES IN CONTEXT.

THIS IS COMPLETELY BASED ON THE INDIVIDUAL, HOWEVER, BELOW ARE SOME SUGGESTIONS JUST IN CASE YOU ARE UNSURE ABOUT WHERE TO BEGIN.

PARTS OF SPEECH, PRESENT TENSE CONJUGATIONS, PERSONAL PRONOUNS, POSSESSIVE PRONOUNS

PRETERIT AND IMPERFECT CONJUGATIONS, REFLEXIVE VERBS, INDIRECT AND DIRECT OBJECT PRONOUNS, FUTURE TENSE, CONDITIONAL TENSE

EL SUBJUNTIVO, FUTURO SIMPLE, CONDICIONAL SIMPLE, CONDICIONAL COMPUESTO

PRO TIP: Take note of the 2 most helpful verb conjugation endings and a few Spanish words you may need to refer back to as you complete this week's prompt

VERB TENSE:		
PRONOUNS:	AR VERBS	ER/IR VERBS
YO:		
TÚ		
ÉL, ELLA, USTED		
NOSOTROS (AS)		
VOSOTROS(AS) SPAIN ONLY		
USTEDES, ELLOS, ELLAS		

VERB TENSE:		
PRONOUNS:	AR VERBS	ER/IR VERBS
YO:		
TÚ		
ÉL, ELLA, USTED		
NOSOTROS (AS)		
VOSOTROS(AS) SPAIN ONLY		
USTEDES, ELLOS, ELLAS		

PARTS OF SPEECH:
N = NOUN
V = VERB
ADV = ADJVERB
ADJ = ADJECTIVE
PREP = PREPOSITION

| JAN | FEB | MAR | APR | MAY | JUN | JUL | AUG | SEP | OCT | NOV | DEC |

1 2 3 4 5 6 7 8 9 10 11 12 13 14 15 16 17 18 19 20 21 22 23 24 25 26 27 28 29 30 31

| JAN | FEB | MAR | APR | MAY | JUN | JUL | AUG | SEP | OCT | NOV | DEC |

1 2 3 4 5 6 7 8 9 10 11 12 13 14 15 16 17 18 19 20 21 22 23 24 25 26 27 28 29 30 31

| JAN | FEB | MAR | APR | MAY | JUN | JUL | AUG | SEP | OCT | NOV | DEC |

1 2 3 4 5 6 7 8 9 10 11 12 13 14 15 16 17 18 19 20 21 22 23 24 25 26 27 28 29 30 31

| JAN | FEB | MAR | APR | MAY | JUN | JUL | AUG | SEP | OCT | NOV | DEC |

1 2 3 4 5 6 7 8 9 10 11 12 13 14 15 16 17 18 19 20 21 22 23 24 25 26 27 28 29 30 31

JAN	FEB	MAR	APR	MAY	JUN	JUL	AUG	SEP	OCT	NOV	DEC

1 2 3 4 5 6 7 8 9 10 11 12 13 14 15 16 17 18 19 20 21 22 23 24 25 26 27 28 29 30 31

| JAN | FEB | MAR | APR | MAY | JUN | JUL | AUG | SEP | OCT | NOV | DEC |

1 2 3 4 5 6 7 8 9 10 11 12 13 14 15 16 17 18 19 20 21 22 23 24 25 26 27 28 29 30 31

WEEKLY CHECK IN

DATE: _____

3 NEW VERBS I LEARNED THIS WEEK:

○ _____
○ _____
○ _____

OVERALL, MY SPANISH FELT LIKE:

A LANGUAGE LEARNING CHALLENGE I HAD THIS WEEK:

NEXT WEEK I WANT TO IMPROVE

_____
_____
_____
_____

THINGS I ACCOMPLISHED THIS WEEK

MY FAVORITE THING I LEARNED THIS WEEK

MY SPANISH WRITING THIS WEEK

★ ★ ★ ★ ★

Week 6: ¡Viva México!

FUN FACT: DID YOU KNOW THAT ¡VIVA!" BEFORE THE NAME OF A COUNTRY IS BASICALLY COMMUNICATING THE DESIRE FOR THAT COUNTRY TO THRIVE AND PROSPER? THINK OF "LONG LIVE" OR "LIVE ON" IN ENGLISH.

THIS WEEK, PRACTICE YOUR READING SKILLS AND LEARN SOMETHING NEW ABOUT MÉXICO! USE THE FOLLOWING RESOURCES AND DOCUMENT WHAT YOU LEARN IN SPANISH IN YOUR JOURNAL PAGES.

- HABLACULTURA.COM (NIVEL A)
- SPANISHBOAT.COM (BEGINNERS READINGS)
- SEARCH: "MEXICAN SPANISH READING FOR ABSOLUTE BEGINNERS" ON YOUTUBE

- RELATOSEHISTORIAS.MX
- HABLACULTURA.COM (NIVEL B)

- MEXICANA.CULTURA.GOB.MX/
- CONCEPTO.DE/CULTURA-MEXICANA/
- DONQUIJOTE.ORG/ES/CULTURA-MEXICANA/

JAN	FEB	MAR	APR	MAY	JUN	JUL	AUG	SEP	OCT	NOV	DEC

1 2 3 4 5 6 7 8 9 10 11 12 13 14 15 16 17 18 19 20 21 22 23 24 25 26 27 28 29 30 31

JAN	FEB	MAR	APR	MAY	JUN	JUL	AUG	SEP	OCT	NOV	DEC

1 2 3 4 5 6 7 8 9 10 11 12 13 14 15 16 17 18 19 20 21 22 23 24 25 26 27 28 29 30 31

JAN	FEB	MAR	APR	MAY	JUN	JUL	AUG	SEP	OCT	NOV	DEC

1 2 3 4 5 6 7 8 9 10 11 12 13 14 15 16 17 18 19 20 21 22 23 24 25 26 27 28 29 30 31

| JAN | FEB | MAR | APR | MAY | JUN | JUL | AUG | SEP | OCT | NOV | DEC |

1 2 3 4 5 6 7 8 9 10 11 12 13 14 15 16 17 18 19 20 21 22 23 24 25 26 27 28 29 30 31

JAN	FEB	MAR	APR	MAY	JUN	JUL	AUG	SEP	OCT	NOV	DEC

1 2 3 4 5 6 7 8 9 10 11 12 13 14 15 16 17 18 19 20 21 22 23 24 25 26 27 28 29 30 31

| JAN | FEB | MAR | APR | MAY | JUN | JUL | AUG | SEP | OCT | NOV | DEC |

1 2 3 4 5 6 7 8 9 10 11 12 13 14 15 16 17 18 19 20 21 22 23 24 25 26 27 28 29 30 31

| JAN | FEB | MAR | APR | MAY | JUN | JUL | AUG | SEP | OCT | NOV | DEC |

1 2 3 4 5 6 7 8 9 10 11 12 13 14 15 16 17 18 19 20 21 22 23 24 25 26 27 28 29 30 31

WEEKLY CHECK IN

DATE: _____

3 NEW WORDS I LEARNED THIS WEEK:
- _____
- _____
- _____

A LANGUAGE LEARNING CHALLENGE I HAD THIS WEEK:

OVERALL, MY SPANISH FELT LIKE:

NEXT WEEK I WANT TO IMPROVE
_____
_____
_____
_____

THINGS I ACCOMPLISHED THIS WEEK

MY FAVORITE THING I LEARNED THIS WEEK

MY SPANISH READING THIS WEEK
★ ★ ★ ★ ★

Week 7: Maná

Maná is one of the best selling Mexican pop-rock bands of all time. One of my go-to albums when I first started learning Spanish was "Revolución de Amor".

This week search Maná on Youtube or your go-to music app and find a few songs to listen to by this band. Write the Spanish lyrics for one or two verses of a different Maná song for each journal entry.

Try to sing along once you learn the lyrics!

| JAN | FEB | MAR | APR | MAY | JUN | JUL | AUG | SEP | OCT | NOV | DEC |

1 2 3 4 5 6 7 8 9 10 11 12 13 14 15 16 17 18 19 20 21 22 23 24 25 26 27 28 29 30 31

| JAN | FEB | MAR | APR | MAY | JUN | JUL | AUG | SEP | OCT | NOV | DEC |

1 2 3 4 5 6 7 8 9 10 11 12 13 14 15 16 17 18 19 20 21 22 23 24 25 26 27 28 29 30 31

| JAN | FEB | MAR | APR | MAY | JUN | JUL | AUG | SEP | OCT | NOV | DEC |

1 2 3 4 5 6 7 8 9 10 11 12 13 14 15 16 17 18 19 20 21 22 23 24 25 26 27 28 29 30 31

| JAN | FEB | MAR | APR | MAY | JUN | JUL | AUG | SEP | OCT | NOV | DEC |

1 2 3 4 5 6 7 8 9 10 11 12 13 14 15 16 17 18 19 20 21 22 23 24 25 26 27 28 29 30 31

| JAN | FEB | MAR | APR | MAY | JUN | JUL | AUG | SEP | OCT | NOV | DEC |

1 2 3 4 5 6 7 8 9 10 11 12 13 14 15 16 17 18 19 20 21 22 23 24 25 26 27 28 29 30 31

| JAN | FEB | MAR | APR | MAY | JUN | JUL | AUG | SEP | OCT | NOV | DEC |

1 2 3 4 5 6 7 8 9 10 11 12 13 14 15 16 17 18 19 20 21 22 23 24 25 26 27 28 29 30 31

JAN	FEB	MAR	APR	MAY	JUN	JUL	AUG	SEP	OCT	NOV	DEC

1 2 3 4 5 6 7 8 9 10 11 12 13 14 15 16 17 18 19 20 21 22 23 24 25 26 27 28 29 30 31

WEEKLY CHECK IN

DATE: _____

3 NEW WORDS I LEARNED THIS WEEK:
- _____
- _____
- _____

OVERALL, MY SPANISH FELT LIKE:

A LANGUAGE LEARNING CHALLENGE I HAD THIS WEEK:

NEXT WEEK I WANT TO IMPROVE
_____
_____
_____
_____

THINGS I ACCOMPLISHED THIS WEEK

MY FAVORITE THING I LEARNED THIS WEEK

MY SPANISH LISTENING THIS WEEK
★ ★ ★ ★ ★

Week 8: Karaoke

¡Esta semana vamos a cantar! This week we are going to sing! I hope you're ready!

It's time for karaoke in Spanish! Search YouTube for three of the following songs by the phenomenal Celia Cruz to learn the lyrics and sing along. Pay special attention to your pronunciation of the lyrics and ways you can improve! Be sure to research what each song is about.

Write the Spanish lyrics to a part of your song choices in the "Letra" section of the provided templates. Next to "Más apuntes"- give a summary of what your chosen song is about.

1. La Cuba Mía
2. La Vida Es Un Carnaval
3. Oye Cómo Va
4. Quizás, Quizás, Quizás
5. Yo Viviré
6. Guantanamera
7. Quimbara
8. La Negra Tiene Tumbao

DIARIO DE CANCIONES

JAN	FEB	MAR	APR	MAY	JUN	JUL	AUG	SEP	OCT	NOV	DEC

1 2 3 4 5 6 7 8 9 10 11 12 13 14 15 16 17 18 19 20 21 22 23 24 25 26 27 28 29 30 31

♪ Canción

Título _____

Cantante _____

Contexto _____

Más Apuntes:

✏ Letra

_____
_____
_____
_____
_____
_____
_____
_____
_____
_____
_____
_____
_____
_____

| JAN | FEB | MAR | APR | MAY | JUN | JUL | AUG | SEP | OCT | NOV | DEC |

1 2 3 4 5 6 7 8 9 10 11 12 13 14 15 16 17 18 19 20 21 22 23 24 25 26 27 28 29 30 31

♪ Canción

Título _____

Cantante _____

Contexto _____

Más Apuntes:

✎ Letra

JAN	FEB	MAR	APR	MAY	JUN	JUL	AUG	SEP	OCT	NOV	DEC

1 2 3 4 5 6 7 8 9 10 11 12 13 14 15 16 17 18 19 20 21 22 23 24 25 26 27 28 29 30 31

♫ Canción

Título
Cantante
Contexto
Más Apuntes:

✎ Letra

| JAN | FEB | MAR | APR | MAY | JUN | JUL | AUG | SEP | OCT | NOV | DEC |

1 2 3 4 5 6 7 8 9 10 11 12 13 14 15 16 17 18 19 20 21 22 23 24 25 26 27 28 29 30 31

JAN	FEB	MAR	APR	MAY	JUN	JUL	AUG	SEP	OCT	NOV	DEC

1 2 3 4 5 6 7 8 9 10 11 12 13 14 15 16 17 18 19 20 21 22 23 24 25 26 27 28 29 30 31

JAN	FEB	MAR	APR	MAY	JUN	JUL	AUG	SEP	OCT	NOV	DEC

1 2 3 4 5 6 7 8 9 10 11 12 13 14 15 16 17 18 19 20 21 22 23 24 25 26 27 28 29 30 31

| JAN | FEB | MAR | APR | MAY | JUN | JUL | AUG | SEP | OCT | NOV | DEC |

1 2 3 4 5 6 7 8 9 10 11 12 13 14 15 16 17 18 19 20 21 22 23 24 25 26 27 28 29 30 31

WEEKLY CHECK IN

DATE: _____

3 NEW WORDS I LEARNED THIS WEEK:
- _____
- _____
- _____

OVERALL, MY SPANISH FELT LIKE:

A LANGUAGE LEARNING CHALLENGE I HAD THIS WEEK:

NEXT WEEK I WANT TO IMPROVE
_____
_____
_____

THINGS I ACCOMPLISHED THIS WEEK

MY FAVORITE THING I LEARNED THIS WEEK

MY SPANISH SPEAKING THIS WEEK
★ ★ ★ ★ ★

Week 9: Arte y Poesía

This week, you will read some poetry written by the renowned Cuban poet, José Martí. Reflect on the meaning of the poetry by writing your thoughts about it in Spanish.

You will then have space to create some art of your own to represent the deeper meaning of a selected verse from each poem.

Poems for this week's prompt:

1. Dos Patrias
2. Cuba Nos Une
3. No Me Quites Las Canas

Find poems online. at:

HTTPS://WWW.POEMAS-DEL-ALMA.COM/JOSE-MARTI.HTM

| JAN | FEB | MAR | APR | MAY | JUN | JUL | AUG | SEP | OCT | NOV | DEC |

1 2 3 4 5 6 7 8 9 10 11 12 13 14 15 16 17 18 19 20 21 22 23 24 25 26 27 28 29 30 31

1. DOS PATRIAS

DRAW OR PASTE AN IMAGE THAT REPRESENTS THE FOLLOWING QUOTE FROM "DOS PATRIAS":

"ESTÁ VACÍO
MI PECHO, DESTROZADO ESTÁ Y VACÍO
EN DONDE ESTABA EL CORAZÓN."

| JAN | FEB | MAR | APR | MAY | JUN | JUL | AUG | SEP | OCT | NOV | DEC |

1 2 3 4 5 6 7 8 9 10 11 12 13 14 15 16 17 18 19 20 21 22 23 24 25 26 27 28 29 30 31

2. CUBA NOS UNE

DRAW OR PASTE AN IMAGE THAT REPRESENTS THE FOLLOWING QUOTE FROM "CUBA NOS UNE":

"CUBA ES TU CORAZÓN, CUBA ES MI CIELO,
CUBA EN TU LIBRO MI PALABRA SEA."

JAN	FEB	MAR	APR	MAY	JUN	JUL	AUG	SEP	OCT	NOV	DEC

1 2 3 4 5 6 7 8 9 10 11 12 13 14 15 16 17 18 19 20 21 22 23 24 25 26 27 28 29 30 31

3. NO ME QUITES LAS CANAS

DRAW OR PASTE AN IMAGE THAT REPRESENTS THE FOLLOWING QUOTE FROM "NO ME QUITES LAS CANAS":

"CADA CANA ES LA HUELLA DE UN RAYO
QUE PASÓ, SIN DOBLAR MI CABEZA."

JAN	FEB	MAR	APR	MAY	JUN	JUL	AUG	SEP	OCT	NOV	DEC

1 2 3 4 5 6 7 8 9 10 11 12 13 14 15 16 17 18 19 20 21 22 23 24 25 26 27 28 29 30 31

| JAN | FEB | MAR | APR | MAY | JUN | JUL | AUG | SEP | OCT | NOV | DEC |

1 2 3 4 5 6 7 8 9 10 11 12 13 14 15 16 17 18 19 20 21 22 23 24 25 26 27 28 29 30 31

| JAN | FEB | MAR | APR | MAY | JUN | JUL | AUG | SEP | OCT | NOV | DEC |

1 2 3 4 5 6 7 8 9 10 11 12 13 14 15 16 17 18 19 20 21 22 23 24 25 26 27 28 29 30 31

| JAN | FEB | MAR | APR | MAY | JUN | JUL | AUG | SEP | OCT | NOV | DEC |

1 2 3 4 5 6 7 8 9 10 11 12 13 14 15 16 17 18 19 20 21 22 23 24 25 26 27 28 29 30 31

WEEKLY CHECK IN

DATE: _____

3 NEW WORDS I LEARNED THIS WEEK:
_____
○ _____
○ _____
○ _____

A LANGUAGE LEARNING CHALLENGE I HAD THIS WEEK:

OVERALL, MY SPANISH FELT LIKE:

NEXT WEEK I WANT TO IMPROVE
_____
_____
_____
_____

THINGS I ACCOMPLISHED THIS WEEK

MY FAVORITE THING I LEARNED THIS WEEK

MY SPANISH WRITING THIS WEEK
★ ★ ★ ★ ★

Week 10: Eltiempo.com

Eltiempo.com is a Colombian website where you can find the latest news about current events in Colombia as well as the rest of the world.

This week, challenge yourself to find and read at least 2 different news articles on this website to learn something new about Colombia. Summarize each article you choose in your journal entries.

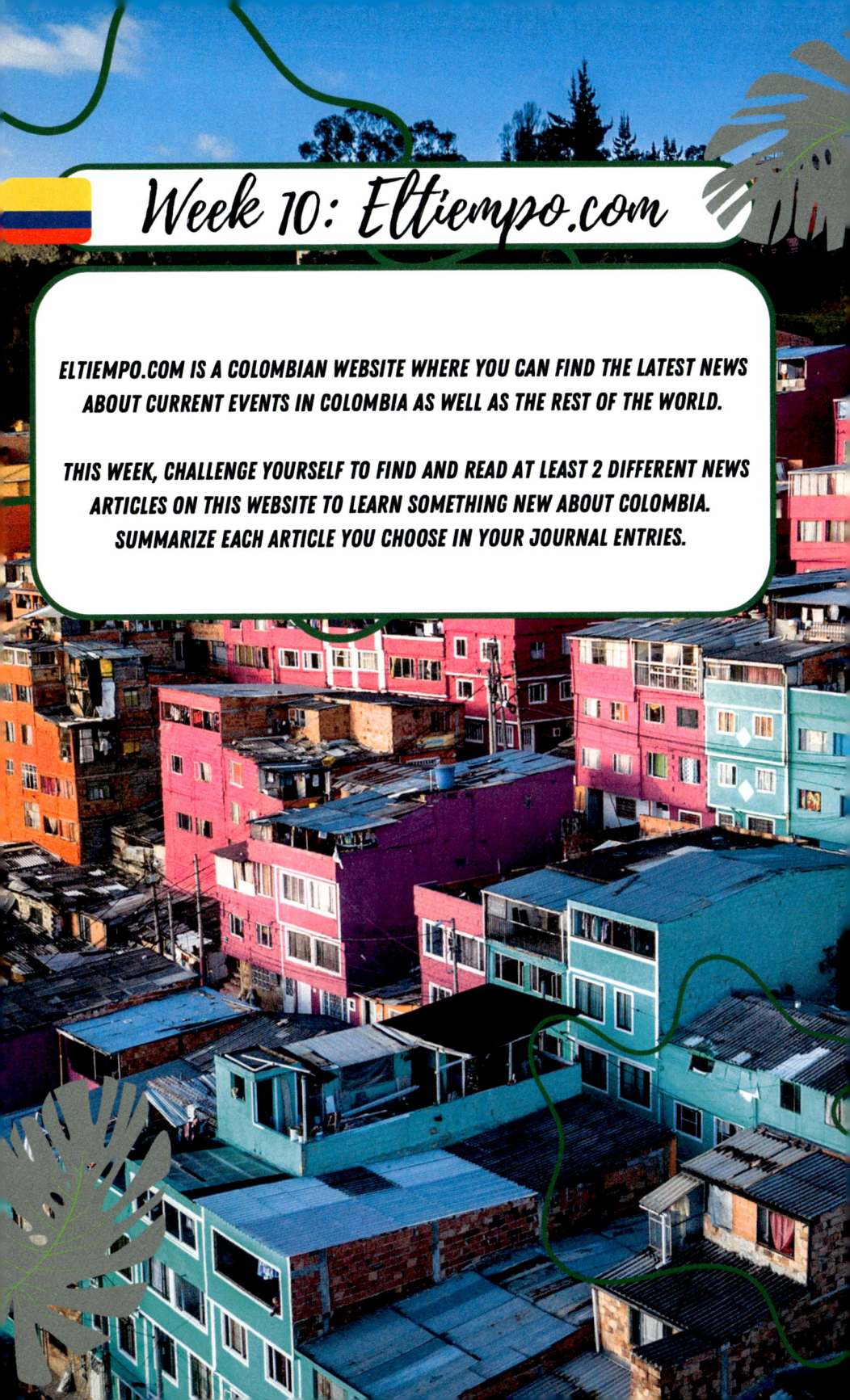

JAN	FEB	MAR	APR	MAY	JUN	JUL	AUG	SEP	OCT	NOV	DEC

1 2 3 4 5 6 7 8 9 10 11 12 13 14 15 16 17 18 19 20 21 22 23 24 25 26 27 28 29 30 31

TÍTULO DEL ARTÍCULO:

AUTOR:

RESUMEN:

JAN	FEB	MAR	APR	MAY	JUN	JUL	AUG	SEP	OCT	NOV	DEC

1 2 3 4 5 6 7 8 9 10 11 12 13 14 15 16 17 18 19 20 21 22 23 24 25 26 27 28 29 30 31

TÍTULO DEL ARTÍCULO:

AUTOR:

RESUMEN:

| JAN | FEB | MAR | APR | MAY | JUN | JUL | AUG | SEP | OCT | NOV | DEC |

1 2 3 4 5 6 7 8 9 10 11 12 13 14 15 16 17 18 19 20 21 22 23 24 25 26 27 28 29 30 31

| JAN | FEB | MAR | APR | MAY | JUN | JUL | AUG | SEP | OCT | NOV | DEC |

1 2 3 4 5 6 7 8 9 10 11 12 13 14 15 16 17 18 19 20 21 22 23 24 25 26 27 28 29 30 31

| JAN | FEB | MAR | APR | MAY | JUN | JUL | AUG | SEP | OCT | NOV | DEC |

1 2 3 4 5 6 7 8 9 10 11 12 13 14 15 16 17 18 19 20 21 22 23 24 25 26 27 28 29 30 31

| JAN | FEB | MAR | APR | MAY | JUN | JUL | AUG | SEP | OCT | NOV | DEC |

1 2 3 4 5 6 7 8 9 10 11 12 13 14 15 16 17 18 19 20 21 22 23 24 25 26 27 28 29 30 31

| JAN | FEB | MAR | APR | MAY | JUN | JUL | AUG | SEP | OCT | NOV | DEC |

1 2 3 4 5 6 7 8 9 10 11 12 13 14 15 16 17 18 19 20 21 22 23 24 25 26 27 28 29 30 31

WEEKLY CHECK IN

DATE: _____

3 NEW WORDS I LEARNED THIS WEEK:
- _____
- _____
- _____

A LANGUAGE LEARNING CHALLENGE I HAD THIS WEEK:

OVERALL, MY SPANISH FELT LIKE:

NEXT WEEK I WANT TO IMPROVE

_____
_____
_____
_____

THINGS I ACCOMPLISHED THIS WEEK

MY FAVORITE THING I LEARNED THIS WEEK

MY SPANISH READING THIS WEEK
★ ★ ★ ★ ★

Week 11: La Reina del Flow

La Reina del Flow is the title of a Colombian telenovela set in Medillín, Colombia. It's the story of a talented, teenaged songwriter who ends up wrongly imprisoned and a seeks justice for the wrongs commited against her and her entire family, 17 years after her release.

This week, watch this telenovela or another Colombian TV series from the list below, according to your personal interests. Search on Netflix or Google to find these titles. Try watching with the Spanish subtitles on.

Journal about new things you learn about Colombian Spanish and culture throughout the week in your journal entries.

La Reina del Flow
Sin Senos Sí Hay Paraíso
Las Muñecas de la Mafia
All For Love
Arelys Henao: Canto Para No Llorar
Locombianos
Juanpis González

| JAN | FEB | MAR | APR | MAY | JUN | JUL | AUG | SEP | OCT | NOV | DEC |

1 2 3 4 5 6 7 8 9 10 11 12 13 14 15 16 17 18 19 20 21 22 23 24 25 26 27 28 29 30 31

| JAN | FEB | MAR | APR | MAY | JUN | JUL | AUG | SEP | OCT | NOV | DEC |

1 2 3 4 5 6 7 8 9 10 11 12 13 14 15 16 17 18 19 20 21 22 23 24 25 26 27 28 29 30 31

JAN	FEB	MAR	APR	MAY	JUN	JUL	AUG	SEP	OCT	NOV	DEC

1 2 3 4 5 6 7 8 9 10 11 12 13 14 15 16 17 18 19 20 21 22 23 24 25 26 27 28 29 30 31

JAN	FEB	MAR	APR	MAY	JUN	JUL	AUG	SEP	OCT	NOV	DEC

1 2 3 4 5 6 7 8 9 10 11 12 13 14 15 16 17 18 19 20 21 22 23 24 25 26 27 28 29 30 31

JAN	FEB	MAR	APR	MAY	JUN	JUL	AUG	SEP	OCT	NOV	DEC

1 2 3 4 5 6 7 8 9 10 11 12 13 14 15 16 17 18 19 20 21 22 23 24 25 26 27 28 29 30 31

JAN	FEB	MAR	APR	MAY	JUN	JUL	AUG	SEP	OCT	NOV	DEC

1 2 3 4 5 6 7 8 9 10 11 12 13 14 15 16 17 18 19 20 21 22 23 24 25 26 27 28 29 30 31

| JAN | FEB | MAR | APR | MAY | JUN | JUL | AUG | SEP | OCT | NOV | DEC |

1 2 3 4 5 6 7 8 9 10 11 12 13 14 15 16 17 18 19 20 21 22 23 24 25 26 27 28 29 30 31

WEEKLY CHECK IN

DATE: _____

3 NEW WORDS I LEARNED THIS WEEK:
- _____
- _____
- _____

OVERALL, MY SPANISH FELT LIKE:

A LANGUAGE LEARNING CHALLENGE I HAD THIS WEEK:

NEXT WEEK I WANT TO IMPROVE
_____
_____
_____
_____

THINGS I ACCOMPLISHED THIS WEEK

MY FAVORITE THING I LEARNED THIS WEEK

MY SPANISH LISTENING THIS WEEK
★ ★ ★ ★ ★

Week 12: Conversación

This week we are back to working on our speaking skills. Our cultural lens is Venezuelan Spanish!

Choose four days this week to take 10-15 minutes to research videos on YouTube about Venezuelan Spanish, according to the suggested context for each entry. Pay close attention to how words are pronounced and practice repeating new words aloud to yourself.

One of my favorite videos for accents is by "Bilingüe Blogs" and it's titled "How to Speak Like a Venezuelan".

If this is too challenging, simply do some research about Venezuelan culture and practice your conversational skills with a friend. Make Venezuelan culture the topic of your conversation.

Remember: It's okay to talk to yourself in Spanish to practice your speaking skills! It's actually necessary to really internalize new information!

Apuntes

> COMPARE AND CONTRAST VENEZUELAN SPANISH WITH OTHER HISPANIC CULTURES YOU HAVE BEEN LEARNING ABOUT. JOT DOWN SOME SIMILARITIES AND DIFFERENCES

JAN	FEB	MAR	APR	MAY	JUN	JUL	AUG	SEP	OCT	NOV	DEC

1 2 3 4 5 6 7 8 9 10 11 12 13 14 15 16 17 18 19 20 21 22 23 24 25 26 27 28 29 30 31

SUGGESTED CONTEXT: VENEZUELAN ACCENT

JAN	FEB	MAR	APR	MAY	JUN	JUL	AUG	SEP	OCT	NOV	DEC

1 2 3 4 5 6 7 8 9 10 11 12 13 14 15 16 17 18 19 20 21 22 23 24 25 26 27 28 29 30 31

SUGGESTED CONTEXT: VENEZUELAN FOOD

JAN	FEB	MAR	APR	MAY	JUN	JUL	AUG	SEP	OCT	NOV	DEC
1 2 3	4 5 6	7 8 9	10 11 12	13 14 15	16 17	18 19	20 21 22	23 24	25 26	27 28	29 30 31

SUGGESTED CONTEXT: VENEZUELAN HISTORY

JAN	FEB	MAR	APR	MAY	JUN	JUL	AUG	SEP	OCT	NOV	DEC
1 2 3	4 5 6	7 8 9	10 11 12	13 14 15	16 17	18 19	20 21 22	23 24	25 26	27 28	29 30 31

SUGGESTED CONTEXT: VENEZUELAN TRADITIONS

| JAN | FEB | MAR | APR | MAY | JUN | JUL | AUG | SEP | OCT | NOV | DEC |

1 2 3 4 5 6 7 8 9 10 11 12 13 14 15 16 17 18 19 20 21 22 23 24 25 26 27 28 29 30 31

| JAN | FEB | MAR | APR | MAY | JUN | JUL | AUG | SEP | OCT | NOV | DEC |

1 2 3 4 5 6 7 8 9 10 11 12 13 14 15 16 17 18 19 20 21 22 23 24 25 26 27 28 29 30 31

WEEKLY CHECK IN

DATE: _____

3 NEW WORDS I LEARNED THIS WEEK:
- _____
- _____
- _____

A LANGUAGE LEARNING CHALLENGE I HAD THIS WEEK:

OVERALL, MY SPANISH FELT LIKE:

NEXT WEEK I WANT TO IMPROVE

_____
_____
_____

THINGS I ACCOMPLISHED THIS WEEK

MY FAVORITE THING I LEARNED THIS WEEK

MY SPANISH SPEAKING THIS WEEK
★ ★ ★ ★ ★

Week 13: Vocabulario

This week, simply focus on internalizing vocabulary in Spanish according to your current level.

Choose three different Spanish words or phrases that you sometimes struggle to recall. Think of those moments where you know you've learned the word you want to say, but it's just not coming to mind. Then when you finally look it up, you think to yourself, "oh yeah, I knew that!"

Fill out the "Palabra del día" templates with your chosen three words. Write the definitions in Spanish.

Reflect on your recollection of how to use these words in context in your last journal entry.

Apuntes

REMEMBER TO IDENTIFY THE PART OF SPEECH FOR EACH NEW WORD. CIRCLE THE CORRESPONDING LETTER ON THE TEMPLATE ACCORDINGLY:

V = VERB
N = NOUN
ADJ = ADJECTIVE
ADV = ADVERB
O = OTHER (WRITE IT IN)

DIA:_____   FECHA:_____

PALABRA DEL DÍA

PALABRA:	IMAGE: DRAW OR PASTE AN IMAGE THAT REPRESENTS YOUR WORD BELOW

DEFINICIÓN
_____
_____
_____
_____

SINÓNIMOS:
_____
_____
_____

ANTÓNIMOS:

PART OF SPEECH: V N ADJ ADV O:

_____
_____
_____

EJEMPLO DE CÓMO SE USA LA PALABRA:
_____
_____

DIA:_____ FECHA:_____

PALABRA DEL DÍA

| PALABRA: | IMAGE: DRAW OR PASTE AN IMAGE THAT REPRESENTS YOUR WORD BELOW |

DEFINICIÓN

_____
_____
_____
_____
_____

SINÓNIMOS:

_____
_____

ANTÓNIMOS:

PART OF SPEECH: V N ADJ ADV O:

_____
_____

EJEMPLO DE CÓMO SE USA LA PALABRA:

_____
_____

DIA:_____ FECHA:_____

PALABRA DEL DÍA

PALABRA:	IMAGE: DRAW OR PASTE AN IMAGE THAT REPRESENTS YOUR WORD BELOW

DEFINICIÓN

_____
_____
_____
_____

SINÓNIMOS:

_____
_____
_____

PART OF SPEECH: V N ADJ ADV O:

ANTÓNIMOS:

_____
_____
_____

EJEMPLO DE CÓMO SE USA LA PALABRA:

_____
_____

JAN	FEB	MAR	APR	MAY	JUN	JUL	AUG	SEP	OCT	NOV	DEC

1 2 3 4 5 6 7 8 9 10 11 12 13 14 15 16 17 18 19 20 21 22 23 24 25 26 27 28 29 30 31

WEEKLY CHECK IN

DATE: _____

3 NEW WORDS I LEARNED THIS WEEK:
- _____
- _____
- _____

OVERALL, MY SPANISH FELT LIKE:

A LANGUAGE LEARNING CHALLENGE I HAD THIS WEEK:

NEXT WEEK I WANT TO IMPROVE
_____
_____
_____
_____

THINGS I ACCOMPLISHED THIS WEEK

MY FAVORITE THING I LEARNED THIS WEEK

MY SPANISH WRITING THIS WEEK
★ ★ ★ ★ ★

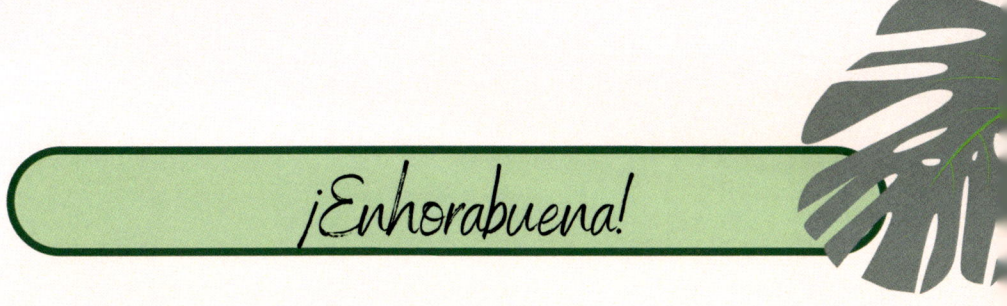

¡Enhorabuena!

CONGRATS ON COMPLETING PART 1 OF THIS GUIDED JOURNAL SERIES FOR SPANISH LANGUAGE LEARNERS! KEEP LEARNING WITH YAPRENDÍ AND OTHER RESOURCES THAT HAVE HELPED YOU ALONG THE WAY. YOU WILL SOON NOTICE HOW MUCH MORE EFFICIENTLY YOU COMMUNICATE IN SPANISH AND HOW MUCH MORE MEANINGFUL YOUR CONNECTIONS BECOME!